STATIONS
OF THE
CROSSED

T0300649

Praise for Stations of the Crossed

"Carol Rose's poetry is profound, phenomenal! The journey of words intertwining takes you to the past and the future. I survived genocide in and from the institutional residential school. I felt the journey, the shift through Carol Rose's incredible poetry. It brought me some tears. This is poetry you want to read again and again. I highly recommend for high school and university classes!"

—Bevann Fox, author of *Genocidal Love*

"I was stripped of any religious or spiritual faith a long time ago. My childhood in Residential School and under the oppressive thumb of the Church proved to me beyond a shadow of a doubt that there is no God or Creator above or around us, for who with such strength and power would allow children to undergo such horror and not step in to save them? The words that Carol has so wonderfully woven together speak to many of the questions I found myself asking over my own life. Juxtaposed with the Fundamentalist Propaganda of the bible, the poems in this collection call out and shine a light upon the truths and pain that we as Indigenous people have faced since the coming of the White Man. They lay bare the ugly reality of the steps taken to erase who we are and what we are, while at the same time questioning the very dogmas and falsehoods pushed upon us as Gospel and Salvation. The underlying theme of Carol's pieces prove one thing emphatically: that our true strength, medicine, and power does not lie with the unseen, omnipotent fallacy of a sky god or ethereal Geppetto-like Daddy Figure, but with the very thing that has not and will never be destroyed, try as they might—the actual living, breathing flesh and blood of us as a people, our mothers and grandmothers and our children, those who have gone before, and those yet to come. Carol's words show where devotion and reverence should be placed; it should be placed upon those who survived the storm, and those who will one day live a life free of the memories of it. This book will speak to those who are needing to hear it, and need to know that it is OK to say, 'wait a minute ...'"

—John Brady McDonald, Nehiyawak-Metis author of *Childhood Thoughts and Water* and *KITOTAM: He Speaks to It*

"*Stations of the Crossed* takes apart this county's long history of trying to extinguish Indigenous culture and the legacy of colonialism. Carol Rose GoldenEagle's own experience as a child of the Sixties Scoop is direct and especially moving. It's been said if we only have one story, that's the story we become. This is a book about finding that new path, and the kind of story we need now—a true one."

—Bruce Rice, author of *The Vivian Poems: The Life and Work of Street Photographer Vivian Maier*

STATIONS
OF THE
CROSSED

POEMS BY

Carol Rose GoldenEagle

Toronto, Ontario, Canada
www.inanna.ca

The publisher gratefully acknowledges the support of the Canada Council for the Arts and the Ontario Arts Council. The publisher is also grateful for the financial assistance received from the Government of Canada.

Cover design: Val Fullard
Cover art: Carol Rose GoldenEagle

Library and Archives Canada Cataloguing in Publication

Title: Stations of the crossed / poems by Carol Rose GoldenEagle.
Names: GoldenEagle, Carol Rose, 1963- author.
Series: Inanna poetry & fiction series.
Description: Series statement: Inanna poetry & fiction
Identifiers: Canadiana (print) 20220415099 | Canadiana (ebook) 20220415102 |
ISBN 9781771339421 (softcover) | ISBN 9781771339438 (EPUB) |
ISBN 9781771339445 (PDF)
Subjects: LCGFT: Poetry.
Classification: LCC PS8607.A5567 S73 2022 | DDC C811/.6—dc23

Printed and bound in Canada

Inanna Publications and Education Inc.
210 Founders College, York University
4700 Keele Street, Toronto, Ontario M3J 1P3 Canada
Telephone: (416) 736-5356   Fax: (416) 736-5765
Email: inanna.publications@inanna.ca Website: www.inanna.ca

I dedicate this book to All My Relations across Turtle Island

CONTENTS

Author's Comments

"What we write may be the very medicine that someone else needs."
— (Carol Rose GoldenEagle, 2018)

In the beginning, I found inspiration to write this manuscript after my son Danny asked a question about why the people of Quebec celebrate Saint-Jean-Baptiste Day. He figured I might know because, as a child of the Sixties Scoop, I was forced to attend Catholic church services each week. Back then, we were taught about the roles of saints. But I stopped going to that church long ago because of its treatment of Indigenous Peoples.

So, I couldn't answer the question asked by my son. Instead, we watched the episode on John the Baptist, which happened to be playing on Netflix at the time, as part of the film series called *The Bible*. I was interested enough to watch the entire series later. Then I borrowed an actual Bible from my neighbour, Mary.

The more I was reacquainted with what I had been taught during my childhood spent in church, the more I realized there are so many parallels between those stories and real happenings within our Indigenous communities. There is inter-connectedness in many ways, which, to me, is often dark and unjust.

So I wrote. I have a great deal of faith, but not in what I was taught about faith as a child. My own Indigenous culture has always held respect to honour the unknown because they (the unseen) are present every day.

For those of you who wonder about the title of this collection, I remember attending church services around Easter as a child. The church held a ceremony called the stations of the cross, where the priest burned incense and walked from plaque to plaque, hanging on the church walls. Each showed a depiction of the stages of Christ's persecution through to his resurrection.

I renamed it *Stations of the Crossed* for this project because I remember an old nun from my childhood who used to always say, "Don't get cross" anytime anyone showed anger or frustration. So to me, the word "cross" means something that causes disruption, imbalance, or negativity, and the crossed are those that have been disrupted, including Indigenous Peoples.

Hence, *Stations of the Crossed*. Indigenous Peoples have a right to re-examine the teachings of the church, and government, and be "cross" about how it has affected our lives. We have been badly treated, historically and still today.

The poems here look back but, more importantly, look forward to reclaiming the gifts, given to us by Creator, within my own rich Indigenous culture.

ABRAHAM

the story says he journeys to an undesignated land
to become the father of a new nation
that was the plight of Abraham   born 2,150 years before the birth of
   Jesus Christ
according to records
one of Abraham's greatest wants   other than pleasing God
is to have a son
who will carry the name Isaac
Hebrew origin meaning   one who rejoices

I understand Abraham's longing

it is more than 2,000 years after the birth of Christ now
and my own son   Jackson   is no longer a boy

I did not name him after a Bible passage   although that book says
   the name means
God has given him the gifts of being gracious and merciful
he has been my reason to rejoice

I knew the very first moment I held my son in my arms
the nurses wanted me to breastfeed
so did I
but before then   I said a prayer to thank God

I held delicate little hands that have since grown strong
I touched his small nose
then ran my hand over a head full of soft black hair
I noticed a little shock of white hair

what does it mean

I think it means he was born holding ancient wisdom
blood memory   handed down by Ancestors
a signal that
in his own way   he too
will be the father of a new Nation

reconciliation
reclamation
renewal

AMAZING GRACE

how sweet the sound
that saved a wretch like me
I once was lost   but now am found
was blind   but now I see
("Amazing Grace," 1772, John Newton, Anglican Clergyman)

Mary Magdalene   Jezebel   Lilith
why is it always the women who are scandalous
in the Bible
or
in real life today

I know these women
filled with light and darkness
both necessary
light and darkness
both teachers

which you feed the most   becomes the strongest

if you spend a childhood   hungry   you steal food
is this a sin
probably not
a crime
according to the justice system

5

you end up a juvenile delinquent

that is not the real you
you are strong   and don't even know it
because you have been listening too long   believing the lies of others
who want to keep you in a place from knowing strength

it is a place you never belonged   child

so you continue and learn to fight   just to stay alive
it is all you have been taught
all you have seen or experienced
a crime or a reality
even if it involves a knife

it brings you to that place of darkness
watching the sadness of others   sitting in a cold cell called the
    drunk tank
you can't help but think
horses have much more power than us
they run free   an innate knowing to run from danger before
    lightning strikes

a reminder that no one
except blood memory
can tell you

you think of the four leggeds   especially the wild ones
survivors   even through all the traps set by man

they know when to flee   how to flee
so do we
it is in our blood   finding the way out of traps
with the guidance of Ancestors   who were banished there before
now
through you Iskwew   those Ancestors urge you to be a winged one
fly   towards the light

darkness is always present   but allow it in only when needed
during those times to avoid another trap
real or imagined

you will find your way out   listening to the whispers of Spirit
   following it

faith
in yourself
and in Creator and those who surround us

carrying the blood of a strong line of women   Iskwew   Nimis   Kohkum
we rebuild
find our way out
forward

HONOUR THY MOTHER

I remember
sitting at the edge of that prairie slough

it smells of promise
watching tadpoles grow   tails   legs   becoming the body of that frog
I put into a Roger's Syrup pail

that slough   a stagnant body of water to some
a place of paradise for this child

watching
as birds sit on skinny branches
willows with soft buds
bull rushes   called a wild cucumber
because you can eat the root

those birds   every colour of a clear rainbow
chirping to each other   signalling
when a crowd of water bugs comes to the surface to breathe
those birds dine

that stagnant body of water   where I went swimming
only to emerge   with legs and arms looking like welts
that were just

hungry bloodsuckers who lived there and attached to me
also wanting to dine

my small pond of memories
where I would search for flat stones   on the nearby grid road
so I could proudly perfect skills
at sidearm throws   skipping stones
and making wishes

I was five years old

One
Two
Three
Four   decades later

I cry
those voices are only in memory

my magic slough   today   a small field of alkali
dried up   cracked   bleeding
forced to carry the effects of a mixture   called chemicals and greed

barren witness
our sad reminder of how we have abused   so much

no frogs
no bugs
no plant life
no bloodsucking slugs
no sound
no laughter

just a cracked   and tortured   dried out piece of land
that not long ago
teemed   with life   promise   memories

and how Creator meant it to be

Honour thy Mother
our Earth

a sad legacy   of how we have treated Her

but   She has been watching
and is speaking now

                              listen

I live to hear the sound of frogs   once more
not just
tell the story to my grandchildren

FATIMA

Our Lady of the Holy Rosary of Fatima
a canon   after seeing apparitions of the Virgin Mary and Angels
Portugal 1917   the vision seen as a prophecy to end World War I
the story prevalent within Christianity

anyone can read about this
suggesting that   *only those who follow in the footsteps of Christ*
  may receive the gift of sight
Fatima in this case
others have been written about in the Bible

but   faith   divinity   believing   holds no dogma
there is a no rule book saying there is only one proper way to pray
nor is there a road map

except for maybe your own heart

do not discount the gifted ones within my own Indigenous culture
they see and converse with Spirit
all the time

it is never written down

but passed on
through words   stories   song
and memory

NOAH

who called you disrespectful   and ingrained that it is sinful to
    question faith
to question what is written in The Good Book

I do it   and I am neither showing disrespect nor being a sinner

here is how I see it

Turtle Island is where we live
others call her North America
Creator began with a cleansing of water   a flooded Mother Earth
    at the start

flooding done
to put an end to the feuding of man

animals survived   Loon   Turtle   Muskrat
because they are without sin   and yes   they do have a soul
everything in creation does

those three were tasked with swimming beneath the flood waters
    to collect soil
to be used to recreate a new world

scholars call it a myth
how would they know

it is gentler to believe that nature took care of herself
minus the meddling   or credit to   the hand of man

our own Creation stories make more sense to me
and
I will keep repeating them

THE FORBIDDEN FRUIT

I tire of Bible words that blame
claiming Eve is responsible for today's chaos

the story says her actions are the starting point for when everything
    went awry

why is this the only story told
to those of my People who still follow the teachings of that Catholic
    church
even knowing
how that church has destroyed   life   language   culture
    community   family

no one has historically documented our own story about the forbidden
    fruit

alcohol

to examine how it has destroyed and disrupted

there is no Indigenous Bible on ways out
towards forgiveness   for ourselves
offering with the same zeal and range of knowing
to even acknowledge or try to understand

14

without blame
without shame

but
the street people and homeless you see   they know
they exist for a reason   and not of their own doing
they are victims of our own forbidden fruit
do some reading

those people regarded as bums do have honour   although masked in
    substance abuse
but their hearts still speak   and dream   and hold blood memory

theirs is not a decision to live like the way they do   couch surfing
    or on cardboard outside
checking garbage cans for food thrown away
maybe even selling their body   because it is the only thing they
    feel they might own

who would make that choice

stop with judgement
this is not your domain

yet they survive   because they have learned how
in a world that has been hard and cruel

I send prayers to keep them safe   and that they find their way out
they walk among us to teach lessons
in kindness   humility   humanity   gratitude   patience

pay attention

these thoughts aside   but related

it was not a woman who introduced forbidden fruit harm to my
    Ancestors
destruction which came in a bottle

it was offered by those early men
intent on stealing for themselves   the Land we roamed
where buffalo ran and fed families
the bottle was the beginning of a sad scene to rape the Land
and the riches offered by Mother Earth

those first contact settlers were not women
they were early men on Turtle Island
who made the word   whiskey
a regular part of the vocabulary   the narrative
back then
and still lingering as part of today's reality

it is easier to cope when you cannot remember

fire water   is what the early Ancestors called it
because fire can destroy
and it has   but not with everyone
and not forevermore
that story needs to come to an end
to be retold
and lived in a different way   which again includes the voices of
    Ancestors
they are waiting

and it will happen
retold with a different outcome
just like the story of the forbidden fruit

the villain is not a feminine
she never was

THE VOICES OF WOMEN

the voices of women
are absent from the Bible

we are the ones who give life
we are the ones who raise the children
within my culture   a long time ago before contact   no decisions
   were made
without the consult of women

matriarchs

a balance upset with the imposition of ideas of those early settlers
those men
who refused   negotiation with the feminine   a sacred Spirit

but that was then

women's voices are now a roar

it is advisable to listen

IDLE HANDS

idle hands are the devil's workshop; idle lips are his mouthpiece
(Proverbs 16:27–29)

here are some names you should remember
            Nina Wilson   Sheelah McLean   Jessica Gordon
    Sylvia McAdam
and
there is nothing idle about their efforts

with hands that nurture
yet are strong
they prepare a recipe
of hope
that feeds a Nation

carrying protest signs
no idle lips
instead raising voices
speaking truths about stopping the devil
through acts of love

idle no more
the strength of women

as our children watch
they learn to follow
to design their own futures
not have one imposed

that time has passed

idle no more
it is no longer just a movement
it is   a way of life

A MOTHER'S HEART

is always open
eyes and ears are too
keeping one hand
within safe and close distance
always there for you   children

Mother Earth feeds us
let us stop treating her bad
polluting our waters
raping everything that she has   just like our women

but when a Mother's heart cries
tears of joy
my heart
watching you learn and grow and accomplish   despite the odds
beautiful baby boy

steering towards what is good in life
protecting from the bad

carry on carry on towards the dance
hear that drum beat   Ancestors speak

we embrace this second chance

at taking our rightful place

THE COMMANDMENTS

the ten commandments are the basis for the law of God

thou shalt have no other Gods but me

> in 1884, the federal government amended the
> Indian Act, banning traditions such as dancing

> *It is with alarm that the holding of dances by the Indians*
> *on their reserves is on the increase, and that these practices*
> *tend to disorganize the efforts which the Department is*
> *putting forth to make them self supporting. I have, therefore,*
> *to direct you to use your utmost endeavours to dissuade the*
> *Indians from excessive indulgence in the practice of dancing.*
> (*Indian Act*, 1921, Duncan Campbell Scott, Deputy
> Superintendent, Department of Indian Affairs)

> *I want to get rid of the Indian problem. Our objective is to*
> *continue until there is not a single Indian in Canada that*
> *has not been absorbed into the body politic and there is no*
> *Indian question and no Indian department.*
> (1921, Duncan Campbell Scott)

thou shalt not steal

The earliest reserves in Canada appear to have been
established on seigneurial holdings by Catholic missionary
orders, dating back as far as 1637, imposing a sedentary
lifestyle on previously semi-nomadic peoples.

The Indian Act of 1876 codified the methods through which
Indian status and reserves were governed by the federal
government.

The nature of the reserve system was the creation of
agreements to forfeit lands and rights.

("Reserves," 2020, *The Canadian Encyclopedia*)

thou shalt not kill

Cowessess First Nation Chief Cadmus Delorme calls on the Pope to apologize after 751 unmarked graves are found on the site of a former residential school in Saskatchewan.

An apology is one stage of many in the healing journey
(2021, Cowessess First Nation Chief Cadmus Delorme)

thou shalt not bear false witness against thy neighbour

First Nations Treaty Commissioner Alexander Morris told
the Cree in 1876

*What I trust and hope we do is not for today and tomorrow
only; what I will promise, and what I believe and hope you
will take, is to last as long as the sun shines and yonder
river flows.*

*In reality, the federal government policy was very different.
The intent was to assimilate.*
("Honuring the Truth," 2015, Truth and Reconciliation
Commission)

the goal of residential school

*We will instill in them a pronounced distaste for the native
life so that they will be humiliated when reminded of their
origin. When they graduate from our institutions, the
children have lost everything native except their blood.*
(Bishop Vital Grandin, 1875)

thou shalt not covet thy neighbour's land

> *To enable the colonization of the Northwest, in 1871, the federal government began negotiating the first in a series of what came to be termed as "Numbered Treaties" with the First Nations of western and northern Canada.* ("Honouring the Truth," 2015, Truth and Reconciliation Commission)

now it is time for me to smudge

WHERE TO FIND GOD

when I ask myself this question
I'm usually alone
worried that others may think
it insane   to travel solo

walking a nearby hillside
there is no burning bush
only wind
soil and grass below me
leaves on trees   waving in unison
asking   what is the rush

Creator knows every movement
each thought   hears prayers   responds to intent

Jesus is coming   look busy
are words that I invent

God lives in my heart
picks me up   in times of need
carries us all to safety
that   is easy to believe

so   look in the mirror
to see the face
of what is real
what is true

answers are all there
no need to search elsewhere

THE BOOK OF JUDGES

Samson   Israelite warrior with great strength
he shall never cut his hair for this is the source

in the end   he was betrayed
enemies cut his hair   he lost his strength
but God restored that strength   so he could continue to fight

Creator is doing the same for us

a single strand of hair is weak   until braided
representing the free flow of life

honour and respect
unity with all our relations   Mother Earth   Father Sky
the four leggeds   the winged ones   those who live under water
plant life   the Spirit world
those we cannot see   but we know they are near

Osawa Mikisew Napew was the spirit name given to him upon birth
the Elders had seen leadership as part of his journey
the name would give him strength and direction
so would his braid

three strands   a connection to things past   present   future
a source of pride and identity and belonging

as Kohkum brushed then braided his hair each morning
before heading out to check the snare wires   with Mooshum
   providing instruction

it was the day Osawa Mikisew Napew turned six years old
when dread arrived
Mounties carrying side arms came right into the kitchen
where the boy was eating some berries
they grabbed him   shoved Mooshum to the side

his last memory of home

later   the large brick building surrounded by a fence was ominous
where had these men taken Osawa Mikisew Napew   and why

women dressed in black forced him out of the car

taking him into that building   that smelled bad

even though Kohkum had taken care to carefully braid his hair again
earlier in the morning
those dressed in black did not like it
they took scissors and cut his braid
telling Osawa Mikisew Napew that his name was now Paul

those pagan names are of the devil   they told him

Osawa Mikisew Napew did not know what that meant

those dressed in black slapped him hard   gave him a broom
and told him to sweep the floor
hard work   you will learn the Lord's ways

as if setting and checking snares   skinning   fishing
and foraging for roots   tubers   and berries   wasn't work
it fed the family

here

those dressed in black forced Paul to eat expired meat that was on
    the verge of rotting

rot

like being imprisoned in a place with bars on the windows

and a fence that keeps children from running through tall grass
    tasting the wind

that was years ago
the memories are hard but carry the knowledge
that he'll do his best to live up to his real name

Osawa Mikisew Napew

and let his own grandchildren grow their braids
he prays for connection to what he knew before those dressed in black
    upset balance

as he stands on a hill top   wearing a braid now the colour of steel grey
he knows
Creator will restore his strength
so he can continue the fight

MISKASOWIN

finding one's sense of origin and belonging,
finding one's self, or finding one's centre
("Treaty Elders of Saskatchewan," 2000, Cardinal and Hildebrandt)

I had been born only one day
when they took me away
leaving my mother to cry
hoping that pride in culture would die

a sinister stage two
of what happened to you
my brothers and sisters who were forced to go to residential school

the hungry jackals had learned
that even with beatings
abuse
starvation
and their lies

your early memories of language
and place   of traditions   and love
stayed within you
stayed alive
there was a hope of returning

it is in those memories you found a place to belong
you carried that song
it made you strong
and able to deflect the shame
that is why the jackals changed course and gave it a different name

the scoop

I imagine the whispers
and how they planned

> *if we get them right at birth*
> *they will have no memory*
> *let us eliminate the anchors*
> *to People and place*
> *assimilate*
> *condition them to adhere to white race*
> *that is how to deal with this Indian problem*

the scoop
it happened to thousands of us
across thousands of miles
made us wards of the state
a wicked plan that went terribly wrong
my love for culture   for place   language has always been carried
nurtured
in places unseen and deep within

the jackals never accounted for
blood memory that is strong
and that Ancestors sing to us all
the moment we are born

> *Awasis*
> *we are here*
> *guiding you back to where you belong*
> *kisakihitin*

my sacred lullabye
that guided me through the storm
words of love to live by
finding the strength to carry on

THE HOUSE OF GOD

the best guess is that the Vatican has financial worth
of 15 billion dollars

so really
what does it cost
to offer an apology

> *for I know my transgressions, and my sin is ever before me*
> (Psalm 51:3)

A HOUSE MARKED WITH BLOOD

Bible stories say   a house marked with lamb's blood
turns away the Angel of Death

who decides
one person's life matters   and another's does not
no Angelic decisions here
only the arrogance and misgivings of man

when a high-profile politician gets so drunk
that he falls in his hot tub   breaking ribs   an ambulance is called
attempts are made   to try to cover up   what happened

the news leaks out anyway
but no one bats an eye
the comments

everyone does that
it happens   he had a little   or a lot   too much to drink
why is this even a story in news
so what

and his life moves forward without consequence or judgement
he is even promoted in his job

when a native woman has too much wine
her worst week on the job site   where her ass was pinched and slapped
even by the foreman   who did nothing

so she fed and settled her kids   then opened a bottle of wine

but the neighbours noticed through her open blinds
an empty bottle on the veranda   and she   with a glass to her lips

they see through the window
and call social services   who arrive with RCMP

they come to apprehend her children   who are asleep in their beds

it is not hushed   as police lights are a beacon to onlookers who gather

the officer tries rushing past a door that shows only a crack
because of a safety chain
the woman slams it   and tries calling a friend
no answer
the menacing knocking continues

they have come to take away her children   who are no longer asleep
she is frantic   and she's had some wine   maybe too much

what started out as a quiet evening at home alone turns into a
a fatally bad decision

her husband is not at home   but his rifle is
he is a hunter
she loads it   pointing it before opening the door

but the crack of the rifle isn't from her
there is no negotiation

she is shot dead on her veranda
as children watch in horror

that home is still stained with her blood
faint markings that remain
right underneath the bundle of sage she tied above her doorway

she picked then bundled the sage with her children
days ago
just before a new school year is to begin
they pick medicines together every summer

honouring the land   honouring spirit   honouring our Ancestors

no one asked her about this
still   Creator knows

the children's new backpacks   filled with school supplies
are by the doorway

it is not likely they will show much interest in learning now
as the social workers lead them past their dead mother's body
laying on the deck and covered under a sheet

that is the reality of a house marked with blood

who decides?

DIVINE SPIRIT

in the most basic sense   a saint is a holy one
   set apart for God's special purposes

our women are then saints
proudly wearing a braid and a ribbon skirt   in place of metal armour

grandmothers   aunties   sisters

divine
woman
for   bringing and sustaining life
prudent
for   being patient   even through the many times of chaos
hope
for   without pause   willfully sacrificing so that others may grow
justice
for   speaking up even when it is difficult to do so   regardless
   of how others may view this
because it is the right thing to do
temperance
for   not allowing the curse of fire water into our homes
it was purposely introduced by those white settlers
to keep us in a fog   with the aim of keeping us in a weakened state
but our women are stronger
courage

for   always standing in the face of danger   countering hatred
   with kindness   slaying down those who wish us to fall but never
   needing to use a sword
faith
for when we walk   a thousand Ancestors help to guide our steps
charity
for it comes in many forms   woman is the first to know   the first to
   offer what is needed

divine spirit
and her name is woman

CROSSROADS

this is what the Lord says: stand at the crossroads and look;
ask for the ancient paths, ask where the good way is, and you
will find rest for your souls
(Jeremiah 6:16)

I stood at those crossroads
feeling guilt   feeling shame   feeling anger
assimilated since the day I was born
Sixties Scoop
taken from my Cree roots
denied my traditions   denied knowing my family   denied my
  own language
raised like a white girl
was told lies   repeatedly   Indians are lazy
                             Indians are drunks
                             Indians are thieves
                             Indians are bad
they were lies I believed as a young girl
it is why I tried to wash off the brown from my own skin

when I grew to be a woman
I met an Elder
she held my brown hand and told me stories
she invited me to come pick sage
she taught me how to sew a ribbon skirt

she encouraged me to dance
and
she was not any of those things   that the white people said

it was the beginning of my own personal Creation story
I learned a few words   *kinanaskomitin*

                                           tansi

                                           kisakihitin

                                           Nikawiy

my tongue was happy
but when I repeated the words   to the white woman who raised me
it was her words that brought me to my crossroads
as she grabbed a bottle of hand sanitizer from the counter and said

                                           here

                                         now you can go and party

                                         next time you see her

I haven't been back there since

        are they ashamed of the abomination they have committed?
no they have no shame at all; they do not even know how to blush
                                 Jerusalem's final warning

DESIDERATA

go placidly amid the noise and the haste   remember what
peace there may be in silence   without surrender be on
good terms with all persons   speak your   truth quietly
and clearly   and listen to others   be at peace with God
(1927, inspired prayer-poet Max Ehrmann)

She is as strong as rock
as fluid and free running as water
and can be just as treacherous if not respected
determined like Mother Earth   to allow continued growth
meant to feed our spirit
feed our children

She has no particular name
only a knowing   that She has the power to make change

She is the one who takes charge
when a daughter or son in trouble is threatened by the system
by mistakes made   not by choice   but by history and
    subsequent circumstance

          You are not able to properly care for your own children

                                        so we

  will apprehend

She goes placidly into the noise to make it right
to find light

She is the one who stands puts her own life and plans on hold again
as a way of restoring balance
those grandchildren will now be raised within the safety of Her arms
Her knowledge
Her pride

not within the system

She
is my grandmother

Kohkum kisakihitin

I lay a soft kiss on her wrinkled cheek
and say a prayer of gratitude

ADAM'S RIB

I call bullshit
a story that keeps saying   God created man
and woman was some sort of afterthought

and why do all those Bible stories imply that God   is a man
why not a woman
or a divine Spirit with no gender

I have great belief in faith and the divine
it defines me   guides me

I prefer our own Creation stories   which do not discriminate

we are all interconnected
all my relations   including Bear   Coyote   Raven   Fish
and those we cannot physically see

we descend from the stars   an important part of the Universe
Creator placed the four leggeds first   because they are truly
   without sin

Muskrat plays an important role   but you will never find that story
   in a textbook
only in the words of our Elders

our Creation stories do not cater to the arrogance of man

it is why I teach my children to question   in every sense   every
    situation
I will do the same for my grandchildren
and
if you consider me a sinner   to embrace these beliefs
spawned in blood memory
I will respond that you are a small-minded asshole
and will dismiss you

renewal

CRUCIFIXION

it is Canada's legacy
our home and Native Land

Native Land
until it was taken away
a brutal history   covered up
the story told in textbooks for youth   sanitized
or not included at all

too many numbers to deal with
too many Ancestors vilified

it was November 27th, 1885
when 8 Native warriors were hanged by the neck until dead
the largest mass hanging in Canadian history

who honours their names now   Wandering Spirit
who shot a priest in a church at Frog Lake

a naked house marked with blood

who will say that Little Bear   Walking the Sky   Bad Arrow   or
    Miserable Man
were wrong in their actions
which resulted in more deaths that day

the Frog Lake Massacre it is known as
those Cree killed people who promised much
then promptly took away
Canadian history doesn't tell the story of   Iron Body   or the Man
    without Blood
and how all were pushed   into taking a stand

the settlers killed the buffalo   knowing the outcome and taking the land

let the People starve   we will withhold food rations
and force them to live like us   or die
heathens either way
we take what is theirs   and never write about it
hope no one ever cares

but the frogs remember
at the lake named after their sound

they remained silent that day   in 1885
large eyes   watching it all   as 8 Native men were publicly hanged
for fighting for things so basic   just wanting their loved ones to stay alive

food   a place to call home   the right to honour Spirit and carry on
    with Traditional ways
love
respect for land and family
honour   to fight for what is real

the frogs have been waiting to retell this story

which is today

remember the names of the warriors who were hanged that day

and move in your own ways

towards also remembering what is real and important   and why these
    men fought

words   the Ancestors say

(Frog medicine reminds us of the transient nature of our lives.
This Spirit Animal supports us in times of change, as well as
symbolizing cleansing)

TRINITY

heralding the teaching of trinity
the Bible says three look out for me
Father   Son   Holy Ghost

here is the story that I like most

Creator does exist
Spirit does exist

guiding us
but wanting us to find our own way
back to what is good

trinity helping to find that path

Nikawiy Mother
Notawiy Father
Kohkum Grandmother

divinity is within us all
in the home   at the kitchen table   by the campfire
a hungry knowing within the heart
now coaxing us to unlearn that the ceremonies of our Ancestors were
    wrong
because they are not held in a church

divinity is creation that sustains
something held by all
the four leggeds have always known
everything holds Spirit

Creator blessed Mother Earth

it is why we sit in her Lodge
and give thanks
for a balance now being returned

FIRE

Iskotiw is how we say it in Cree
the word for fire

it is what fuels us
sustains us
keeps us alive
keeps us warm
enables us to cook our food
feed our families
tell stories around the fire
celebrate life

fire

it comes from a sacred place
Iskwew   meaning woman
Otih   meaning heart

our home fires are the heart of woman
a place where we build   family   friendship   community
all that is real

damn you   Catholic Church for calling my language pagan
and slapping my Ancestors for speaking truth
even putting pins in tongues   for speaking Cree

you fucking savages   black robed nuns and priests and
    social workers
did your best to silence us

Creator knows   not the God you forced us to bow to in your Church

so we continue with fire

woman has kept it alive
the heart of woman
the heart of all that is good
the heart of humanity   is woman

even Jesus would rejoice
in the fire that will forever burn within the heart of woman
and the children we are blessed with   who carry on and build
    or rebuild

fire
the voice of woman was never silenced   never taken away

woman   ours holds the spirit of generations
fire
that is woman
and this is where we start again

Iskotiw

SUNDOGS

he waits for me every afternoon
that skinny puppy
gulping down the bannock and lard
that I sneak from the counter
even though Nikawiy forbids it

then we run
summertime
and down to the lake
into the bush
every night he sleeps under the stairs outside
because Nikawiy will not let him in the house
even though
he is my closest friend

that skinny puppy
Nitotem

months later
a blizzard howls

Nitotem is bigger now
as the wind slashes him with pellets of hard snow
Nitotem crouches by the doorway
as I watch
through the small bit of window where I scratch off the frost

a heart softens that night
as Nikawiy watches me cry
she finally opens the door and lets him in

by springtime
he is still with me
this time sleeping on my bed instead of under the stairs

my close friend
Nitotem
we run and play every day
he watches over my safety
especially that day a badger runs towards me
Nitotem distracts it
while I head for home

he is good that way

but Nitotem cannot help me
the day that black car comes to a stop
while I am out catching tadpoles in a puddle beside the ditch

he tries
while those men grab me hard
pulling my hair and forcing me into the back seat
they club Nitotem over the head with a shovel from their trunk
when he bares his teeth and snarls at them

57

I watch and sob
as my friend is left by the side of that road
bleeding

those men in that black car take me to a place
with cold granite floors and foul smells

all the people there wear black
the colour of their souls
their mean eyes watching every movement

until
one winter afternoon

that nun leaves us alone
in front of that hard brick building
after a kid falls on ice and smashes his nose

it is so cold out
still I run and run and run
until my lungs feel heavy

when I collapse into fresh snow
I feel warmth
looking up toward the sundogs

Mooshum always says
sundogs signal change

but I think it is Nitotem
this time in the sky
still watching out for me
helping me find the way home

before closing my eyes
I study the colours of those sundogs
the rainbow of frozen tears
and think of Ancestors guiding me now

refracting the empty blackness
of what I escape

BREAD OF LIFE

Jesus said, I am the bread of life. Whoever comes to me
will never go hungry.
(John 6:35)

1942 to 1952
1,000 First Nations children in residential school
are intentionally starved
the government of Canada sanctioned the experiments
withholding food
to study the effects of a poor diet

one of those effects included the beating of a child
many children
little Serenity knows this

the nuns gave her that name the day she arrived at residential school
it means peace
but that is not what Serenity found there

being slapped in the classroom   for falling asleep at her desk
being kicked while on kitchen duty   she was too weak to lift that
     heavy pan
being shaken at the dining table   for no longer being able to
     stomach what was set before her
it happened just after the priest uttered those words again before eating

I am the bread of life

Serenity died in her sleep that night and was buried in an unmarked
grave

intentional starvation is murder

OUR DAILY BREAD

Give us this day our daily bread
forgive us our trespasses
lead us not into temptation
deliver us from evil
(the Lord's Prayer)

ever eaten bread so stale that it is beginning to turn mouldy
it leaves a foul taste that memory cannot erase

that is the story for my relations
Nikawiy went to the Sturgeon Landing residential school
she hardly talks about what happened there
but her silence says a lot
as does her body language when the place is mentioned

she suffers from diabetes   like so many others in my family
that is a result of that place too
the kids were starved
their growing bodies damaged to the point that   it can not properly
    process
now as an adult

forgive us our trespasses   were the empty words uttered by the
    priests and nuns
just before dining on steak and fresh produce

Nikawiy remembers   because they forced her to work in the kitchen
she served them heaping plates
just before going back to the common area
where the kids ate soup   that was more tasteless broth than
  anything of substance
it was served   alongside a piece of daily bread

FOOD

If you are willing you will eat the good things from the land
(Isaiah 1:19)

we did
and then it was killed
taking sad pictures of a pile of bones in Regina
dead buffalo
like it was something to rejoice

and our land where berries   roots   and tubers grew
have been plowed under
four leggeds   like caribou   are sent off the path they have travelled
  since the beginning of time
so companies can drill for oil
fish die in polluted waters

our children continue to be hungry
eating only mac and cheese or canned soup from the Food Bank

we were always willing to eat good things from the land

Mother Earth did provide
been abused
and now corporate villains can no longer hide

POWDERED MILK

not even 50
and already in need of hip replacement surgery
sparking so many questions

did you have a bad accident somewhere
does it run in your family
do you suffer some type of disease

yes   yes   and yes
though not the way you might think

definitely it can be seen as a bad accident
except
replace the word accident with circumstance
it was real for too many families
and racism is a disease that is contagious

it is called the scoop

but bureaucrats do not refer to its real name
too harsh to say kidnap
punishment
genocide
too real for too many families

and where my powdered milk story begins

it was the faux families who benefitted
as a ward of the state   foster families took us in

so often to them
it meant only extra income
and
free labour

hush
you go sleep in the barn
unless the social worker comes
you cannot sit at our table
there is a good enough outhouse behind the shed
here is an old coat with only a bit of fray on the sleeves
should keep you warm enough
no extra mittens though
you can always use your pockets

foster care
a system that lived up to only half its name
there was no caring
only shame

eating the scraps from leftovers
if we were lucky
but mostly we might only expect a meal

of thin oatmeal
covered with the rusty nail taste of powdered milk

small bones need calcium to grow strong
otherwise
expect a hip replacement in later years

the memory of that time remains
but now I view the scar from where that weak bone was removed
as a badge of survival

I am still here

INTO THE WILDERNESS

> *Jesus was led by the Spirit into the wilderness to be tempted*
> *by the devil.*
> *After fasting 40 days and 40 nights   he was hungry*
> *The temptor came to him and said*
> *If you are the Son of God   tell these stones to become bread*
> *Jesus answered*
> *It is written   Man shall not live by bread alone*
> *but on every word that comes from the mouth of God*
> (Matthew 4:1–11)

Mooshum takes his grandson Little Bear   into the wilderness
  every day
there
Little Bear is taught
how to fish   gut   skin
taught
how to snare   and give tobacco
showing gratitude to the animal who gave up life   so the family
  can eat and be sustained
with bow and arrow   Mooshum teaches
and   Little Bear becomes skilled at hunting birds
same   tobacco offering   then a meal
eaten with fresh wild potatoes and mushrooms
that Little Bear's Kohkum teaches him how to identify

they take only what they needed from the Land
Little Bear learns well

so   trying to understand the reason why Indian Agents and
    RCMP would just
bust into their small log cabin one day
take Little Bear away
pushing Mooshum to the floor
Kohkum was crying

those white men were lying   he will be back for a visit at Christmas
then they forced Little Bear out the door

Little Bear arrived at a place that smelled bad   bleach
but never enough can be used to get rid of the smell

there were no fences back then   so Little Bear ran away
back to where his roots are firmly planted
back to memories that save a soul

Kohkum cries   when Little Bear arrives   cold   hungry   dirty
she feeds him   neckbones and her heart strings   and she holds
    him close

but   they don't feel the same about Little Bear at that school

he is just a number there   and a source of income

so when he isn't found   during morning roll call
a roll call like being in prison
those Indian Agents go to capture him again   not only wanting
   his body   but his spirit
which they can never understand   is too resilient and proud to ever
   give away

they burst into the little cabin   grab Little Bear by the collar of
   his shirt
they can't grab his long braid anymore   that   was cut off
they swear at Mooshum
before leaving   they threaten Mooshum   then write a letter

Last winter   an Indian took his child away from the school
            without permission
   This Indian is in receipt of a monthly ration
   which I have ordered that the ration be cut entirely
   until the child is back in school
   (July 24, 1935, Indian Agent N.P. L'Heroux)

our 40 days and 40 nights
have been 40 years   and 40 years   and 40 years   and 40 years
   and 40 years
we still hunger
but we continue to pray   to Creator   the Ancestors
   the Spirit Beings
not to who the Church slapped us into believing   their ways

we have found our way back to each other
and will continue to grow

but   Little Bear   no one knows what happened to him
he never came home from that school   ever

and Mooshum's heart   never healed

I BEG OF YOU

so many forgotten
referred to now only as Sixties Scoop Survivors

residential school was an atrocity
but so is what happened to us

residential school kids had each other   as much as was allowed
brothers and sisters separated in the same forlorn place
but still allowed to catch glimpses   in the schoolyard or that sad
   place called a dining room

those scooped spent a childhood in schoolyards being beaten
teachers knowing and doing nothing
foster parents knowing and not caring   we were a source of income
not welcome

the only glimpses of faces were white   and never smiling

and in my dining room
I was fed powdered milk

CORINTHIANS

Love is patient and kind. Love is not jealous or boastful or
proud or rude. It does not demand its own way. It is not
irritable, and it keeps no record of being wronged. It does
not rejoice about injustice but rejoices whenever the truth
wins out. Love never gives us, never loses faith, is always
hopeful, and endures through every circumstance.
(1 Corinthians 13:4–7)

I never fully understood the teachings of Jesus Christ
until I met an Old Woman
four foot ten
reminds me of Yoda
and just as wise

she has never been sentenced to jail
but she has done hard time
beaten to the point of death in residential school
internal bleeding
the nuns did not send her to hospital until the next day

there
she lay in a coma
for eleven months

but she does not dwell on it
does not empower those early years
fraught with a litany of woe
peppered with hate
a mix of fear

she has not allowed it to hinder her growth
towards becoming
the Old Woman who stands here

proud
strong
courageous

too many now rely on her strength
which has become their starting place
of a shared sacred space
because of this Old Woman

who
years ago
accepted the unspeakable pain that arrived
when her young husband passed too soon

it was then two voices showed up
both promising something

spirits
which come in a bottle
and the Spirits
of the Old Voices we hear in the wind

her husband was gone
their love remained
so she promised
to never drown those memories
but to keep their love   alive and powerful
honouring the memory of her husband
by honouring Spirit   the Old Ones

                                        transformation

smudging with sage   sweetgrass   cedar
she offers prayers for her children
for all children
and a promise that she will embrace
the rhythm of life
no matter what it may bring

it leads her to the circle
that magic place
peaceful place   the church forbade
for no good reason

triumphant
Old Woman stands with an Eagle feather fan
held high at the honour beat
in a dance honouring her

Creator knows
she has earned the respect
towards her role as an Elder
as she continues to beckon
influence
encourage as many as she can
back to the dance
ancient
but new to those who have been disconnected
as she once was
but is no more

it is going on now   3 generations
this dance
getting stronger
and happening
because she let go of pain
felt it
but let it die
remembering instead   the love
a heart so large
it caused rebirth

resurrecting with it
traditions
the Old Ways
and extending that knowledge to her children
grandchildren   great grandchildren

determined
they will not suffer the same
pain
disconnection
wandering in darkness
no more nuns threatening a bad beating

that was a long time ago

BONES

finally the church has released death records
included
are infants who died
while at residential school

not children
records of dead infants
some as young as days old or even just minutes old

how did babies die at residential school

stories have long been told about rape at those schools
new life was the result
priests truly were fathers

but those births would reveal too many secrets
make it go away
smother the cries
cover it up

bury those innocent bones
quickly
without ceremony
hide them in the back hills
and never speak of this again

those bones are speaking now

MIRACLES

I have no idea why there is this notion that miracles need to be
   something grand
for people to believe

miracles   happen everyday
all life is divinely inspired

quiet yourself
abandon expectations
you will see

the rain tells a story when she falls
parched earth renewal
giving life to plants and animals   and us
a miracle and gift

a child takes the first step   towards a lifetime of building and
   rebuilding
grandparents celebrate 50 years of marriage
a family meal
walking the dog
learning to skate
graduating high school   university
quiet moments
moments of challenge

a friendly greeting
finding a feather   or a coin
the sound of music
a God-given gift   in a language that not everyone understands
but responds to
it prompts smiles
which makes the Little People dance
our invisible Spirit protectors   with you all the time

Christianity refers to them as Guardian Angels

I like our stories better   which do not always have to be talked about
nor marked with a statue

just experienced
acknowledged
and appreciated

the active practise of a Teaching in humility

MEEK

blessed are the meek
for they shall inherit the earth
(Jesus in Matthew 5:1–12)

meek equates   gentle quiet easily imposed upon   submissive

an uttered blessing

or more   a quiet threat   historically

speaking we were never quiet   submissive

instead

believing in honour   when a person makes a promise   it will happen

Ancestors   who sacredly held a place in the heart where words
   are not empty

and promises hold meaning

but we were lied to
placing our trust in places unsafe

                    as long as the grass grows   and the rivers flow
                                1876 Treaty promise

later

presented with gifts of blankets

containing smallpox

later

imprisonment on land that is not desirable   to new settlers
swampland where nothing grows   or so they thought
our spirit never died   even through repeated attempts to do so

they called it a reserve   where no one can leave without government
   permission

the pass system

they killed the buffalo

wanting people to starve

not knowing Ancestors still guide

not submissive enough

so   they try to break spirit in other ways
taking our children
not understanding that is our strongest part

they call it a residential school

again   the lies   no honour   only torture

where children are raped   beaten

called dirty   pagan   sinners

tongues pierced   for speaking our languages

which we know   connects us to Spirit   to Creator

too much has happened

and we are still here

rebuilding   reclaiming   lost pieces of ourselves

Ancestors always speak to us   children of generations long passed

the Ancestors come in dreams   or as voices in the wind

telling of ways to undo   rebuild from broken promises

the grasslands are disappearing
we all suffer the plagues predicted   wildfires   drought   a virus
   sent to cleanse

the waterways polluted with the filth of greed

Mother Earth is crying

the meek shall inherit the earth

more like

what's left of it
so much has been destroyed

except for our love   hope   Ancestors knowledge

and our footprints

which will be prominent again

and not in the form of petroglyphs

ECCLESIASTES

For everything there is a season, a time for every activity under heaven.
A time to be born, a time to die. A time to plant and a time to harvest.
A time to kill and a time to heal. A time to tear down and a time to build up.
A time to cry and a time to laugh. A time to grieve and a time to dance.
A time to scatter stones and a time to gather stones.
A time to embrace and a time to turn away. A time to search and a time to
quit searching.
A time to keep and a time to throw away. A time to tear and a time to mend.
A time to be quiet and time to speak. A time to love and a time to hate.
A time for war and a time for peace.
(Ecclesiastes 3:1–8)

good passage
but there was no good time to kill all the plains buffalo
no good time to force sterilization of our women to cull out those
considered unfit by white people
unmarked graves at residential schools
forcing children to work instead of the promise that they would learn
at residential school
so many have been killed   MMIWG
a false Treaty promise of education our schools are funded at 1/3 less
and it is almost impossible to secure post-secondary funding

too much negative on which to reflect
but we do speak now   hear our voices
the time for war and hate is over
our children are in need of our strength

and Jesus is my cousin   hiy hiy

JOHN THE BAPTIST

a figure credited with bridging ideas
the conduit for a strengthening of faith
the link between old and new Testaments

again, Jesus my cousin, why is it only men did anything significant

no disrespect but everyone knows water is the source of life
it's where you lived those nine months before birth
protected by the comfort of
woman's body

the story of John
thank you for reminding us of the importance of water
all water is sacred

let us remember this when some company starts drilling and polluting
or Nestlé stealing and draining   with government approval for profit

Jesus, my cousin, knows
another time for cleansing is near

all water is sacred   let's treat her that way

THE BOOK OF GENOCIDE

in the beginning when God created the heavens and the earth
the earth was a formless void and darkness covered the face of
the deep
(Genesis 1:1–3)

why is it called the Queen City   Regina
whose queen
and what did she do for us First Nations except agree to
steal our land   our lives our children

and we are all now forced to drive in this city   to drive down
    one of its main roads
this city honours the memory of Edgar Dewdney
a major roadway named after someone who agreed with forced
    starvation
of our children in those wicked places

names matter

so pull down statues of frauds who must have known in their hearts
what they did was wrong
but probably they didn't care   more money for them
    and the families who now live with
dirty inherited money while so many still starve

the devil lives here on earth   we elect them
they live in your neighbourhood and you do their yardwork
and no one says
a word

and we continue driving down Dewdney Avenue

BARREN   BARON   BEARING

Her name was Sarah
or so the Bible says
the wife of Abraham   who lived in anguish because she longed for
but couldn't conceive a child
barren
until the day   Archangels showed up giving her the news
that she would be the mother of a new nation   and that she would
　　have a son
God promised   and delivered
a child named Isaac was born   and those stories are passed on

where did that Bible God go when a new nation   supposedly
　　discovered

it is impossible to believe that the Universe would decree that some
　　matter
and others do not

we matter

my people have always lived here   in rhythm with nature and all that
　　surrounds
our daughters and sons are just as sacred
but those stories are not told in the history books
not taught in school

when that first Baron crossed the pond   intent on conquer
he couldn't have known   he would be close to death
not by anyone's hand
but because the Land itself was trying to expel the cancer that would
    later come
poisoning rivers   raping Mother Earth of her abundance

Go back to the reserve   is what those early Indians should have said
instead
saving that Baron and his men from scurvy
teaching that plant life sustains life

years later
that same plant life is ripped from Mother Earth
to make way for uranium and oil
brutal
imposing their way   saying our women do not matter
we deal only with men   selling the lie
the beginning of imbalance

years later
even forcing the sterilization of our women
because women hold medicine that is sacred and strong

Spirit can be crushed   but never killed
that is the heart of woman
bearing children   a new generation
correcting imbalance and guarding

we are

the mothers of a new nation

which will prominently include   the voices of our daughters

FOR YOU HE WILL SPLIT THE ROCK

Elijah
he came from a small place in northern Manitoba
a boy   running through the bush   fishing in clear water
listening to the music that is our Cree language
knowing the strength of the language which connects to the Ancestors

then they took him too   government   the church
forced attendance at residential school
where things happened   to everyone   that he never spoke about
    publicly

trauma   associated memories
it caused some trouble later in his life
but more so   allowed him to find strength and meaning
and a resolve to do his part to never let genocide happen again

Manitoba's first elected Indigenous member of the legislature
generations applaud your strength

the Bible says Elijah was a prophet and a miracle worker who lived in
    the northern kingdom

our Elijah was from Red Sucker Lake   a northern paradise
in 1990
his courage was both miraculous and prophetic

Canada was trying to do it again
repeat a sad and unjust history
rewrite the rights of peoples   leaving Indigenous behind
not even including us as people who have rights
wanting to legislate again   like we are still living in the 1800s

Canada called it the Meech Lake Accord   which needed unanimous
    approval from all legislatures
across the land
Turtle Island   our land   our home   our renewed history

through death threats and scorn   Elijah held strong
holding up his Eagle feather to say
no
we belong
always have
I do not agree to my People being excluded

Creator was with him in those moments   so were the Ancestors and
    all our relations
in history classes with young people today
a name that everyone should know is

Elijah

WILD FLOWER

don't ever transplant a wild flower
she will never mend
never bend

most beautiful in her natural state

let that time end
where you need to control

HEBREW

can't say I know any of the People
can't know if they might know me and mine

Biblical Hebrew refers to the language of ancient Israel
10th century before Christ

meaning no disrespect to the People or that culture and faith
I have to wonder
why use a word that starts with
He

language
holds power

which brings me to something totally unrelated

menopause

all have come to accept it is a biological condition women experience
    in later years
but why that name

men   pause to love us   as we enter a era of wisdom

a word game

rules require   skill   compassion   understanding   patience

STONING

the standard form of punishment in ancient Israel

but is it ancient

it still happens today

similar circumstance

but given a different name

Oka
Ipperwash
Dudley George
Connie Jacobs
Neil Stonechild
Colten Boushie
Helen Betty Osbourne
Tina Fontaine

> *He that is without sin among you, let him cast the first stone*
> (Jesus in John 8:7, King James Bible)

SOME BIBLE TEACHINGS

so much is written
so much to ponder or to be said
so much for which to be embraced   or disagreed

but remember the words of advice that urge   take heed
the Bible talks about this need

there is one universal   God   called by many other names
I say Creator
makes sense to me

Creator the one power
with wise advice for everyone   Kohkum   Mooshum   daughter
  son

take heed

                       beware of false prophets,
                       which come to you in sheep's clothing,
                       but inwardly they are ravening wolves
                       (Matthew 7:15)

permission
to question faith   question teachings   question the actions of others
even in my own Indigenous culture
there will be those who call themselves holy

our Lodges are sacred   and newly allowed only

for it was 1951
when the pass system was repealed
allowing us to practise in our own way
allowing for celebration   and to feel

a rebirth of old ways

but in doing so   be aware and take care

there are those who walk among us   holding themselves out
  as gifted
they will be the first to tell you this

and those of us   previously disconnected because of residential
  school or other
will want to believe
we hunger

but take heed   for his name may be jackal
with jagged teeth   speaking words untrue
and with a jagged heart hidden from view
even though he may carry an Eagle feather

trust yourself
you will know

carrying blood that holds the memory to recognize

if this feeling happens   that something is awry
listen   pray to the Ancestors   raise your voice to the sky

Spirit can see   they know   that false prophets   profit

so seek guidance   in the old ways

your heart will know

holding this courage to question
re-embracing
and learning in a good way
the strength of our Nations   will grow

SEVEN

a child of the Sixties Scoop
and every Sunday forced to go to catechism
those Bible classes   designed specifically for children
held in the cold church basement
that smelled of mould
the sink in that downstairs bathroom had a leak

a ruler smacking my hand
one time   after getting caught fidgeting with a rubber band
stuffed in my pocket

the nun was grey   her dress   her hair   her skin
so was that class
pontificating   about the seven deadly sins

that was a long time ago
I have since met my real family

Kohkum tells a better story about seven

she tells it
while going for a walk in the bush

she says the 7-spotted lady bug is magic
that each spot

is a reminder
of the seven sacred teachings

Love   truth   honesty   respect   humility   wisdom   courage

when Deer appears
Kohkum says   she holds wisdom   sensitive and strong
always trusts her instincts   ensures she's never wrong

walking further   and Coyote shows himself
Kohkum says truth is the gift Coyote brings
he has deep magic and is a teacher of hidden wisdom

humility   is how Kohkum describes Cat   over there   climbing
    a tree
she has balance   action   observation
and understands something about everything she sees

little Fox is watching
Kohkum says   Fox represents honesty
a great guide when facing tricky situations   but mostly   Fox
    follows her dreams

when Raven flies overhead
Kohkum says   she is guided by respect for her surroundings
she is fearless and full of flexibility

but most of all
it is Eagle we love
she flies highest in the sky
Eagle is our connection to higher truths above

seven sacred teachings

Mother Nature reminds us how to be
a guide to live by

makes way more sense to me

WHOSE MIRROR IMAGE

so many differing beliefs in faith around the world
but in Canada
ours was the only one vilified

told there is only one proper way to pray
tortured into believing   God has white skin
        angels   blond hair

it is not taught that Jesus likely had   brown eyes
        black hair
        a darker colour of skin

his eyes are darker than wine
(Genesis 49:12)

maybe he was Cree
with teachings that apply to anyone   everyone
no matter skin colour   history   geography

dogma   equals   damage
which can be repaired

but only with an open heart
and the elimination of barriers   preventing one from moving forward

KNEELING

All are called to acknowledge the Lord's rule in our lives
by kneeling before him in worship
(Psalm 95:6)

our Elders
Knowledge Keepers
our sentinels for what heals spirit   through stories told
                                   teachings and traditions passed down
                                        weathering storms
                                           brought by history

the woman I trust and follow goes by the name of Emily
Latin for rival and persuasive
she is my rock   but never expects to rule me
smiling as she gently encourages me to dance   to drum
  to speak   our Cree language
gentle   when she corrects my ideas   altered ways of thinking
              because of the Sixties   Scoop
              or correcting my Cree pronunciations so it sounds
                 like the music it is
kind   because she knows my own past
respects   that I long to move into the present
she will help
guided by knowledge of the Ancestors   who always watch over me

in honouring her
I honour the Spirit of all our Elders
all those who came before me
all those who endured   sacrificed   rode through pain so we
   would not have to

all my relations

none expect me to kneel before them
only to learn
and pass on the teachings

MIYO-MANITOWI-KISIKANISIK

Merry Christmas
here is how you would be greeted by a Cree

if I was alive in Biblical times
Jesus and I would have been good friends
we still are
but from afar
because the Catholic Church has claimed the season
and doesn't like the way
I pray
even though sweetgrass and sage are sacred to me

Miyo-Manitowi-Kisikanisik
a time for giving and receiving
love   laughter   family   story

here is one filled with glory
and meaning

Miyo-Manitowi-Kisikanisik
not just a day for Christians
but absolutely a day to honour kindness

his name was Charlie
a local street bum
was never able to erase what residential school had done

those nuns and priests had taken his confidence
but never his courage
never shook his kindness
despite all he had seen

he came to the city as a young man
but with only a grade eight education
he wandered
until becoming an Old Man

with no home
in winter he slept at the shelter each night
Salvation Army
when they had a bed
in the summer he slept on the grass by the water's edge
resting in the arms of Mother Earth

he walked the streets every day
greeting everyone with a smile
opened doors for young mothers with strollers
talked to Raven
took his meals at the Salvation Army when they served
although sometimes people would give him money
so he could buy some soup at a store somewhere
and let another street person have his chair
at the shelter

it is why he was so affected when the news came
the Salvation Army folks who cared for him
would be moving away
there was a feast planned to thank them
Charlie went that day

at an open microphone people lined up to say
best of luck
you will be missed
thank you for all you have done

Charlie went further

he reached in the pockets of worn-out jeans
finding a few dollars
that people had given
so he could buy himself coffee or tea

those Salvation Army people had showed him kindness
no matter the season
he was a man with no money
except for today

Charlie did not give a speech
he simply said
here is ten dollars
go buy yourself a nice meal when you arrive at your new home

Miyo-Manitowi-Kisikanisik
the spirit of why we celebrate
no matter the season

WHEN AFTER CHRIST IS NOW

I have been writing this poetry manuscript for more than 2,000 years

they burned my words for speaking up   back then
they burned me

but fire is my friend
she cleanses
getting rid of old dead wood
making way for new growth

mine is not a questioning of faith
for that is our foundation

my people know faith
we know love   and strength   and stories
          and rebuilding
in places that are not contained to a building

it is a time for rebirth

reclaiming a path which follows
what blood memory has always known
since the beginning of time

ACCEPTANCE

we need to accept the past
in order to move on towards a healthy future

> *My people will sleep for 100 years*
> *but when they awake*
> *it will be the artists who give them their spirit back*
> (1885, Louis Riel)

words of hope uttered in sincerity hold power
but only if believed   and acted upon

we are awake now

REFLECTIONS OF GRATITUDE

Nichanis
she was born in 1997
because of that I was able to

make sure she was breastfed
shed tears of joy on her very first day of school
be the first to teach her how to drive
teach her how to make fluffy bannock
be there to celebrate when she earned a gold medal in cross country
    running
head to garage sales where there are no used items   only treasures
    to be found
strap on my skates   hoping to keep up with Nichanis now that she
    is faster
cry together when watching sad movies
laugh together when the dog does something funny
walk together to the lakefront ice cream shop on a hot summer day
tell stories about the days when there were only two channels on the
    television
and there was no such thing as a bank machine   we had to stand in
    line waiting for a teller
dance with her at pow wows
help her pay for her studies at university
watch her progress as she becomes proficient in learning the Cree
    language
make plans for a remarkable future filled with promise and love

so many people remark that Nichanis and I are alike
but I know
that is only partly true

it is the passage of time which has allowed for my warm memories
some say those changes have come too slowly
I am just grateful they came at all

because if she was like me
and born in 1963
I would have missed all those moments

it is because they would have come
and taken her away

Nichanis is the reason
I must turn my heartbreak
into hope   promise   new beginnings

Acknowledgements

As with all my writing, I seek the advice and comments of others before revising that first draft. For this input, I give thanks to Faye Arcand, Carol Wright, Marlyn Keaschuk, Joely BigEagle-Keequatooway, John Brady McDonald, Yasuko Thanh, Waubgeshig Rice, Daniel Lockhart, Bruce Rice, Terri Boldt, Bevann Fox, Betty Tomasunos Sellers, Jackson Adams, Kathy Daley, Mary Donison, Jenelle McArthur, Janice Montgrand, Chelene Knight and for the generous support of this project to the Canada Council for the Arts.

Please note that the poem "Corinthians" is a rework of a poem previously published, entitled "Lilly" and published within the manuscript *Hiraeth* (Inanna Publications, 2017).

For more information on my work, please visit my website at www.carolrosegoldeneagle.ca

Credit: Megan Talaga

Cree/Dene writer and artist **Carol Rose GoldenEagle** was appointed Saskatchewan's Poet Laureate in 2021. She is the author of the award-winning novel *Bearskin Diary*. It was chosen as the national Aboriginal Literature Title for 2017. The French language translation, entitled *Peau D'ours*, won a Saskatchewan Book Award in 2019. Her first book of poetry, *Hiraeth*, was shortlisted for a 2019 Saskatchewan Book Award. Her second novel, *Bone Black*, was shortlisted for both the 2020 Rasmussen & Co. Indigenous Peoples' Writing Book Award (Saskatchewan Book Awards) and Muslims for Peace and Justice Fiction Book Award. Carol's latest novel, *The Narrows of Fear (Wapawikoscikanik)*, won the 2021 Rasmussen &

Co. Indigenous Peoples' Writing Award (Saskatchewan Book Awards), and her poetry collection *Essential Ingredients* was shortlisted for the 2022 SK Arts Poetry Award. Carol was also recently honoured with the Saskatchewan Order of Merit. *Stations of the Crossed* is Carol's third poetry collection.

A visual artist, her work has been exhibited in art galleries across Saskatchewan and Northern Canada. A CD of women's drum songs, Squaw'kin Iskwewak Wymyns' Songs, in which Carol is featured, was nominated for a Prairie Music Award. Before pursuing art on a full-time basis, Carol worked as a journalist for more than 30 years in television and radio at APTN, CTV, and CBC. She lives in Regina Beach, Saskatchewan. www.carolrosegoldeneagle.ca

Also by Carol Rose GoldenEagle

Poetry

Hiraeth
Essential Ingredients

Fiction

Bearskin Diary
Bone Black
Narrows of Fear (Wapawikoscikanik)